CHRIST *in the* CAROLS

CHRIST

⹀ *in the* ⹀

CAROLS

CHRISTOPHER *and* **MELODIE LANE**

TYNDALE HOUSE PUBLISHERS, INC.
WHEATON, ILLINOIS

Visit Tyndale's exciting Web site at www.tyndale.com

Designed by Julie Chen and Jackie Noe.

Library of Congress Cataloging-in-Publication Data

Lane, Christopher A.
   Christ in the carols : meditations on the Incarnation / Christopher and Melodie Lane.
      p.   cm.
   Includes bibliographical references.
   ISBN 0-8423-3521-8 (hardcover : alk. paper)
   1. Carols, English—Texts.   2. Incarnation Meditations.   I. Lane, Melodie, date.   II. Title.
BV530.L36   1999
242′.33—dc21   99-31844

Printed in the United States of America

05   04   03   02   01   00

7   6   5

The central miracle asserted by Christmas is the Incarnation.
They say that God became Man. . . . If the thing happened,
it was the central event in the history of the Earth.

—C. S. Lewis, *Miracles*

CONTENTS

INTRODUCTION

What do you think of when you hear strains of "Hark! the Herald Angels Sing" or "Joy to the World"? Christmas, of course. These and many other beloved carols play a central role in our yearly celebration of Christ's birth. We sing them together in our churches, radio stations add them to their regular fare in December, and shopping malls pump orchestrated versions into stores to get their patrons "into the spirit." It just wouldn't be Christmas without Christmas carols.

Though most of us can recite the lyrics to our favorite carols from memory, we sometimes fail to appreciate their messages. It isn't that their themes are confusing or mysterious. Most are simple songs. The problem is that we have heard them over and over since childhood and become so familiar with them that we tend to take their content for granted. It is easy to sing them each year without really listening to what they are telling us.

Historically, music of the church has been a source of education and inspiration, teaching us about God and encouraging us to worship him. Christmas carols are no different. Some speak of deep theological truths concerning the mystery of the Incarnation. Others offer scriptural descriptions of the events surrounding Jesus' birth. Still others are joyful expressions of childlike faith in response to God's indescribable gift. Together these songs provide us with a poetic lyrical picture of what Christmas is all about. When examined in light of Scripture, they enable us to more fully comprehend, experience, and respond to the miracle of Christ's birth.

In this book we invite you to take a fresh look at a number of carols and let them become a source of holiday meditation, a vehicle for drawing you closer to Jesus. It is our hope that as you take time out of your busy holiday schedule to engage in these devotions, you and your family will be filled with the same awe, wonder, and joy which inspired the songwriters to pen these carols.

The goal in practicing devotions is to devote oneself

to the purpose of fellowshiping with God. With that in mind, consider the following pages as an opportunity to spend time alone with the Lord, to talk with him, wait upon him, worship him, and bask in his presence. If after reading these devotions you are more intimately acquainted with the one whose birthday we celebrate, this book will have achieved its purpose.

Our prayer is that God will reveal to you the incredible truth and life wrapped up in the holiday we call Christmas.

A WORD ABOUT CAROLS

The origin of the word carol is unclear. Some sources believe that it was derived from *choros*, the Greek word for dance. Others argue that it comes from *carole*, a French word that also describes a type of dance, often performed to the music of a flute. In either case, carols seems to have been associated in some way with celebration. During the Middle Ages when church music consisted solely of Latin plain-song performed by ecclesiastical professionals, carols became popular among common folk. They were easy to sing, often expressed joy, and were usually suitable for dancing. It has been suggested that St. Francis, in his attempt to provide popular songs of praise in the language of the people, was responsible for the creation of the first Christmas carols.

The term carol came into modern use in England where it was used to describe a "lyrical poem" which addressed Christmas, Epiphany, Easter, and other events in the Christian calendar. The English carol adhered to specific rules of structure, usually being made up of stanzas which alternated with a short repeated refrain. Over the years more carols were written about Christmas than any other Christian holiday, causing them to become associated almost exclusively with this season. In recent times this once narrow category of songs has been broadened to include nearly every "song of joy or praise" sung at Christmas, no matter its structure.

We have followed the contemporary definition in

selecting the carols for these meditations. Although some are true English carols, most are traditional hymns, songs, and choruses that have become a part of our yearly holiday celebration. Lyrics to some carols differ according to various translations. The renditions reprinted here were selected not because they are the most common or the most authentic but because they best suit the devotional purposes of this book.

SILENT NIGHT

JOSEPH MOHR, 1818

Silent night, holy night,
All is calm, all is bright;
Round yon virgin mother and Child,
Holy Infant, so tender and mild,
Sleep in heavenly peace,
Sleep in heavenly peace.

Silent night, holy night,
Shepherds quake at the sight,
Glories stream from heaven afar,
Heavenly hosts sing, "Alleluia!"
Christ, the Savior, is born!
Christ, the Savior, is born!

Silent night, holy night,
Son of God, love's pure light,
Radiant beams from Thy holy face,
With the dawn of redeeming grace,
Jesus, Lord, at Thy birth,
Jesus, Lord, at Thy birth.

Perhaps the best known and most widely sung of all the carols, "Silent Night" was born out of necessity. As the story goes, Joseph Mohr, the assistant priest of St. Nicholas parish church in Oberndorf, Austria, wrote this song when the organ malfunctioned on Christmas Eve in 1818. Had he not penned these famous lines and persuaded organist Franz Grüber to set them to music for guitar and voice, the service that evening would truly have been silent.

Though the town of Bethlehem may have been relatively quiet when Jesus was born, it was probably not silent. Crowds of weary travelers were constantly arriving to be counted in the census. They walked the streets searching for places to stay, grumbling as they were turned away from the inn. Tired children whined, women with aching feet complained. And even in the stable where Mary and Joseph took refuge, the donkeys and cows would have continued to produce a variety of grunts and snorts.

Mohr's song speaks not of a natural silence. It captures a moment of peace, a holy hush that surely settled over Bethlehem as all of heaven viewed with wonder the birth of the God/Man. The Potter had entered into the clay that he himself had made, and he now rested in the arms of his own creation.

REFLECTION

Because the Christmas season is so hectic and rushed, we often find it difficult to identify with the "holy hush" of that night. But Scripture implores us to make a practice of pausing from our daily routine—in all seasons—to wait upon God and to listen for his still small voice. As Fredrick William Faber once explained, "Whenever the sounds of the world die out in the soul, or sink low, then we hear the whisperings of God."

Read and pray through the following verses. Ask the Lord to draw you into the awesome silence of his presence and whisper his truth in your ear.

"Go out and stand before me on the mountain," the Lord told him. And as Elijah stood there, the Lord passed by, and a mighty windstorm hit the mountain. It was such a terrible blast that the rocks were torn loose, but the Lord was not in the wind. After the wind there was an earthquake, but the Lord was not in the earthquake. And after the earthquake there was a fire, but the Lord was not in the fire. And after the fire there was the sound of a gentle whisper.

1 KINGS 19:11-12

The Lord is wonderfully good to those who wait for him and seek him. So it is good to wait quietly for salvation from the Lord.

LAMENTATIONS 3:25-26

I am counting on the Lord; yes, I am counting on him. I have put my hope in his word.

PSALM 130:5

Be silent, and know that I am God! I will be honored by every nation. I will be honored throughout the world.

PSALM 46:10

PRAYER

Lord, I invite your Spirit to come upon me and calm my busy mind. Quiet my heart as I wait before you. In the silence let me hear you. In the stillness let me know you. Open my eyes that I may see your glory and receive the grace you have extended to me today.

COME, ALL YE SHEPHERDS

BOHEMIAN FOLK SONG
TRANSLATED BY MARI RUEF HOFER, 1912

Come, all ye shepherds, ye children of earth,
Come ye, bring greetings to yon heavenly birth.
For Christ the Lord to all men is given,
To be our Saviour sent down from heaven:
Come, welcome Him!

Hasten, then, hasten to Bethlehem's stall,
There to see heaven descend to us all.
With holy feeling, there humbly kneeling,
We will adore Him, bow down before Him,
Worship the King.

Angels and shepherds together we go,
Seeking this Saviour from all earthly woe;
While angels, winging, His praise are singing,
Heaven's echoes ringing, peace on earth bringing,
Good will to men.

This Bohemian folk song is a call to worship. Notice the writer's gentle but stirring invitation in the first stanza—come, come, come, welcome him. He repeatedly exhorts us to drop what we are doing and turn our attention to the Savior.

Similarly, in the second stanza we are invited to see heaven descend. What should be our response to the human manifestation of almighty God? Holy awe, humility, prostrating ourselves in adoration. This is how a king is to be worshiped.

Jesus no longer walks the earth as a man. Yet the Spirit is moving across the earth, drawing those who are weighed down with woes. Like the shepherds in this carol, we are called to join our voices with the angels, proclaiming peace to a world of violence and strife, goodwill in a land of hatred, bitterness, and despair. The Father is fashioning his people into a responsive chord, that we may ever echo the message of heaven: Jesus is Lord!

REFLECTION

Psalm 100 is a minitreatise on worship. It tells us how God expects us to behave as we approach him. As you read it, invite the Spirit to provide insight into how it should apply to your life. Act out the directives. Ask God for the freedom and boldness to do what the psalmist calls for.

Shout with joy to the Lord, O earth! Worship the Lord with gladness. Come before him, singing with joy. Acknowledge that the Lord is God! He made us, and we are his. We are his people, the sheep of his pasture. Enter his gates with thanksgiving; go into his courts with praise. Give thanks to him and bless his name. For the Lord is good. His unfailing love continues forever, and his faithfulness continues to each generation.

PSALM 100

PRAYER

Father, I accept your call to worship. Teach me how to enter your gates, how to act in your courts. And as I spend time in your presence, fashion me into an instrument of proclamation, that my voice might join the angels in sharing your Good News to a dying world.

GOD REST YE MERRY, GENTLEMEN

ENGLISH TRADITIONAL, EIGHTEENTH CENTURY

God rest ye merry, gentlemen,
Let nothing you dismay,
Remember Christ our Savior
Was born on Christmas Day;
To save us all from Satan's power
When we were gone astray.

O tidings of comfort and joy,
Comfort and joy,
O tidings of comfort and joy.

In Bethlehem, in Jewry,
This blessed Babe was born,
And laid within a manger,

11

Upon this blessed morn;
The which His mother Mary
Did nothing take in scorn.

From God our Heavenly Father,
A blessed angel came;
And unto certain shepherds
Brought tidings of the same:
How that in Bethlehem was born
The Son of God by Name.

The title and first line of this familiar carol are often misunderstood. The lyrics are not referring to a group of merry gentlemen. Instead, they are actually a prayer of blessing addressed to gentlemen. "God rest ye merry" was an old English expression which petitioned God to keep one merry or joyful. "God bless you with joy, you gentlemen" might be an accurate modern-day rendering of the phrase.

It stands to reason that those who are already merry would have no need of such a blessing. Rather it is the lonely and sorrowful, those who are "dismayed," who require comfort. To those in such need, the writer of this carol prescribes the only sure cure—the good news of Jesus.

In singing "God Rest Ye Merry, Gentlemen," we are verbally extending God's blessing, his power to encourage and refresh, to the oppressed. In listening to it, we are afforded the opportunity to receive that blessing, and with it, his joy.

REFLECTION

Is there something in your life which is robbing you of joy? Are you in need of comfort? As you read the following verses, remember that they are true and faithful words from God to you.

All praise to the God and Father of our Lord Jesus Christ.
He is the source of every mercy and the God who comforts us.
He comforts us in all our troubles so that we can comfort others.
When others are troubled, we will be able to give them
the same comfort God has given us.

2 CORINTHIANS 1:3-4

May our Lord Jesus Christ and God our Father, who loved us and in his special favor gave us everlasting comfort and good hope, comfort your hearts and give you strength in every good thing you do and say

2 THESSALONIANS 2:16-17

The Lord your God has arrived to live among you. He is a mighty savior. He will rejoice over you with great gladness. With his love, he will calm all your fears. He will exult over you by singing a happy song.

ZEPHANIAH 3:17

You will show me the way of life, granting me the joy of your presence and the pleasures of living with you forever.

PSALM 16:11

PRAYER

How I long to know the joy and the pleasure of your presence. Lord, draw me close and let me rest in your arms. Hold me, refresh me, renew me in your love.

4

NOW SING WE, NOW REJOICE

TRANSLATED BY ARTHUR T. RUSSELL, 1851

Now sing we, now rejoice,
Now raise to heaven our voice;
Lo! He from whom joy streameth,
Poor in the manger lies;
Yet not so brightly beameth
The sun in yonder skies!
Thou my Saviour art!
Thou my Saviour art!

Given from on high to me,
I cannot rise to Thee:
O cheer my wearied spirit:
O pure and holy Child,

Through all Thy grace and merit,
Blest Jesus! Lord most mild,
Draw me after Thee!
Draw me after Thee!

Now through His Son doth shine
The Father's grace divine:
Death over us hath reigned
Through sin and vanity:
The Son for us obtained
Eternal joy on high.
May we praise Him there!
May we praise Him there!

O where shall joy be found?
Where but on heavenly ground?
Where now the angels singing
With all His saints unite,
Their sweetest praises bringing
In heavenly joy and light:
May we praise Him there!
May we praise Him there!

This old Latin hymn is an overview of the Christian walk. In the first stanza the writer tells of Jesus' birth and welcomes him as Savior. In the second stanza he recognizes Jesus' identity and commits to following after him. Next he recounts what Jesus has accomplished, ending in an exhortation to praise. Finally he looks forward to the joys of our heavenly home. Salvation, discipleship, worship, the hope of eternal life—these are the fundamentals of the Christian faith.

REFLECTION

It is helpful to make a practice of returning to the basics in our life with Christ. These foundational pillars help support our faith when we face various challenges and hardships. As you examine each of the passages listed below, allow the Word to renew your mind and perspective. Use these verses to reaffirm your commitment to Jesus.

God decided to save us through our Lord Jesus Christ, not to pour out his anger on us. He died for us so that

*we can live with him forever, whether we are dead or
alive at the time of his return.*

1 THESSALONIANS 5:9-10

*Jesus said to his disciples, "If any of you wants to be my follower,
you must put aside your selfish ambition, shoulder your cross,
and follow me. If you try to keep your life for yourself, you will
lose it. But if you give up your life for me, you will find true life."*

MATTHEW 16:24-25

*Dear brothers and sisters, I plead with you to give your bodies
to God. Let them be a living and holy sacrifice—the kind he will
accept. When you think of what he has done for you, is
this too much to ask?*

ROMANS 12:1

*The Lord himself will come down from heaven with a
commanding shout, with the call of the archangel, and with the
trumpet call of God. First, all the Christians who have died will
rise from their graves. Then, together with them, we who are still
alive and remain on the earth will be caught up in the clouds to
meet the Lord in the air and remain with him forever.*

1 THESSALONIANS 4:16-17

PRAYER

Jesus, I confess again today that you are my Savior. Even as I celebrate your earthly birth, I commit myself to following you. Draw me in your steps. Keep my eyes focused on you alone. May I live to the praise of your glory.

IT CAME UPON A
MIDNIGHT CLEAR

EDMUND H. SEARS, 1850

It came upon a midnight clear,
That glorious song of old,
From angels bending near the earth
To touch their harps of gold;
"Peace on the earth, good will to men
From heaven's all-gracious King."
The world in solemn stillness lay
To hear the angels sing.

Still through the cloven skies they come,
With peaceful wings unfurled;
And still their heavenly music floats
O'er all the weary world;

Above its sad and lowly plains
They bend on hovering wing,
And ever o'er its Babel sounds
The blessed angels sing.

Yet with the woes of sin and strife
The world has suffered long;
Beneath the angel strain have rolled
Two thousand years of wrong;
And man, at war with man, hears not
The love song which they bring:
Oh, hush the noise, ye men of strife,
And hear the angels sing.

O ye beneath life's crushing load,
Whose forms are bending low,
Who toil along the climbing way
With painful steps and slow;
Look now, for glad and golden hours
Come swiftly on the wing;
Oh, rest beside the weary road
And hear the angels sing.

For lo! The days are hast'ning on,
By prophets seen of old,
When with the ever-circling years
Shall come the time foretold,
When peace shall over all the earth
Its ancient splendors fling,
And the whole world give back the song
Which now the angels sing.

Notice the adjectives employed in this familiar carol: solemn, weary, sad, lowly, crushing, painful . . . These words depict a people who are burdened, bent low by the "woes of sin and strife," and forced to toil over each step. Edmund Sears was obviously describing the plight of fallen mankind. To put it in the modern vernacular, "Life is hard and then we die."

But Sears offers an antidote for the dreary existence of fallen man. "Look now," he implores, "for glad and golden hours come swiftly on the wing; Oh, rest beside the weary road and hear the angels sing." This is not a trite exhortation to "cheer up" or "keep a stiff upper lip." The message which the angels delivered was wrought with hope. "Peace on earth," they proclaimed, "Good will to men . . ." It was news that the Answer to life's questions and problems had come to earth. The Power of God now walked among men. Present was the one who could free them from the burden of sin, who could enable them to know joy and peace.

One day all of creation will join in that song, lifting praise to the Prince of Peace. But we don't have to wait until the second advent of Christ. We can begin singing today, celebrating the first advent, anticipating his second coming, and sharing the news with those who are downtrodden.

REFLECTION

The peace of Christ is available today. As you read the following verses, ask Jesus to give you rest and to show you how to live in the freedom he has provided.

Jesus said, "Come to me, all of you who are weary and carry heavy burdens, and I will give you rest. Take my yoke upon you. Let me teach you, because I am humble and gentle, and you will find rest for your souls. For my yoke fits perfectly, and the burden I give you is light."

MATTHEW 11:28-30

I am leaving you with a gift—peace of mind and heart. And the peace I give isn't like the peace the world gives. So don't be troubled or afraid.

JOHN 14:27

Don't worry about anything; instead, pray about everything. Tell God what you need, and thank him for all he has done. If you do this, you will experience God's peace, which is far more wonderful than the human mind can understand. His peace will guard your hearts and minds as you live in Christ Jesus.

PHILIPPIANS 4:6-7

PRAYER

Lord, I lay my worries, my hurts, and my sins at your feet. They are much too heavy and painful for me to bear. I am crushed beneath their weight. Free me, heal me, and forgive me according to your grace. Breathe your life into my soul, your peace into my heart. Let me find my rest and life in you.

6

COME, THOU LONG-EXPECTED JESUS

CHARLES WESLEY, 1744

Come, Thou long-expected Jesus,
Born to set Thy people free;
From our fears and sins release us;
Let us find our rest in Thee.

Israel's Strength and Consolation,
Hope of all the earth Thou art;
Dear Desire of every nation,
Joy of every longing heart.

Born Thy people to deliver,
Born a child, and yet a king,
Born to reign in us forever,
Now Thy gracious kingdom bring.

By Thine own eternal spirit,
Rule in all our hearts alone;
By Thine all-sufficient merit,
Raise us to Thy glorious throne.

For centuries God had promised to send his anointed one to rescue Israel. The Scriptures were filled with prophecies of his coming kingdom, his power, and his love. But there had been silence for nearly four hundred years—no sign, no word.

Some had grown weary of waiting, their faith eroded by the passage of time. Others remained hopeful, watching, wondering as the years slowly slipped by. They read about him, looked for him, and prayed for his arrival.

This carol by Charles Wesley captures the deep yearning the Israelites must have felt as they awaited Messiah's day. How they longed for their Strength and Consolation to appear. How they hoped to see the Desire of nations arise.

Looking back, it is difficult for us to fully appreciate their sense of anticipation. Yet we find ourselves in a similar situation. When Jesus left, he promised to return, and after some two thousand years, we continue to await that joyous event. Even as we celebrate his birth, we too lift our voices to cry, "Come, Thou long-expected Jesus."

REFLECTION

The Bible says that faith is "being sure of what we hope for and certain of what we do not see" (Hebrews 11:1, NIV). We can be sure that Jesus will come again soon to establish the fullness of his kingdom on the earth. Though we cannot see it yet, we know that day is swiftly approaching.

Let us run with endurance the race that God has set before us. We do this by keeping our eyes on Jesus, on whom our faith depends from start to finish. He was willing to die a shameful death on the cross because of the joy he knew would be his afterward. Now he is seated in the place of highest honor beside God's throne in heaven.

HEBREWS 12:1-2

First, I want to remind you that in the last days there will be scoffers who will laugh at the truth and do every evil thing they desire. This will be their argument: "Jesus promised to come back, did he? Then where is he? Why, as far back as anyone can remember, everything has remained exactly the same since the world was first created." But you must not forget, dear friends, that a day is like a thousand years to the Lord, and a thousand years is like a day. The Lord isn't really being slow about his promise to return, as some people think. No, he is being patient for your sake. He does not want anyone to perish, so he is giving more time for everyone to repent.

2 PETER 3:3-4, 8-9

He who is the faithful witness to all these things says, "Yes, I am coming soon!" Amen! Come, Lord Jesus!

REVELATION 22:20

PRAYER

Jesus, as I eagerly anticipate your return, I invite you to come now and reign in my life. I ask that your eternal Spirit would rule in my heart. Usher me into your glorious presence by your grace and favor, that I may worship before your throne.

7

GOOD CHRISTIAN MEN, REJOICE

TRANSLATED BY JOHN M. NEALE, 1853

Good Christian men, rejoice,
With heart and soul and voice;
Give ye heed to what we say:
Jesus Christ is born today.
Ox and ass before Him bow,
And He is in the manger now.
Christ is born today!

Good Christian men, rejoice,
With heart and soul and voice;
Now ye hear of endless bliss:
Jesus Christ was born for this!
He hath ope'd the heavenly door,

And man is blessed evermore.
Christ was born for this!

Good Christian men, rejoice,
With heart and soul and voice;
Now ye need not fear the grave:
Jesus Christ was born to save!
Calls you one and calls you all
To gain His everlasting hall.
Christ was born to save!

Though the origin of this carol is unknown, its message is clear. In each stanza it urges us to rejoice, and to do so with all of our being and faculties. Like the ox and ass who are portrayed as bowing before the newborn Christ, the writer asks us to humble our hearts before the King. He invites us to celebrate the finished work of Jesus upon the cross, which literally "ope'd the heavenly door" and won our salvation.

Think of it. We have been rescued from the tyranny of death and sin. Those evil taskmasters no longer rule over us. They have been vanquished, conquered, defeated. We who once were in bondage to sin and so afraid of death have been set free to serve a God who is slow to anger, full of mercy and compassion. Jesus is our new master, and love is the new law by which we live. That news not only causes our hearts to rejoice, but gives us good reason to shout the gospel to the world around us. As the writer of this carol exhorts, may we evermore proclaim that "Jesus saves!"

REFLECTION

To rejoice literally means to "see joy," or to be delighted. The joy that this song asks us to see is Jesus. He is the source and object of our joy, for in him we find our delight. No matter our circumstance, Jesus, our joy, is ever present, never changing. Therefore, we will always have reason to rejoice.

The Bible commands us to rejoice on numerous occasions. Read through the following verses with an eye toward understanding this activity. Ask yourself this question: What does it mean to rejoice in the Lord? Then read them again, intent on obeying them.

Be happy in your faith and rejoice and be glad-hearted continually—always.

1 THESSALONIANS 5:16, AMP

Let all those who take refuge and put their trust in You rejoice; let them ever sing and shout for joy, because You make a covering over them and defend them; let those also who love Your name be joyful in You and be in high spirits.

PSALM 5:11, AMP

Be glad in the Lord, and rejoice, you righteous—you who are upright and in right standing with Him; shout for joy, all you upright in heart.

PSALM 32:11, AMP

Rejoice in the Lord always—delight, gladden yourselves in Him; again I say, Rejoice!

PHILIPPIANS 4:4, AMP

I will praise You, O Lord, with my whole heart; I will show forth (recount and tell aloud) all Your marvelous works and wonderful

deeds! I will rejoice in You and be in high spirits; I will sing
praise to Your name, O Most High!

PSALM 9:1-2, AMP

PRAYER

Father, the gift of your Son has made my heart glad! This day, no matter what I encounter, I will choose to look to you and "see joy." With all my heart, mind, soul, and strength, I will rejoice and celebrate your goodness. You alone are my delight, my all in all.

8

As with Gladness Men of Old

WILLIAM C. DIX, 1860

As with gladness men of old
Did the guiding star behold;
As with joy they hailed its light,
Leading onward, beaming bright;
So, most gracious God, may we
Evermore be led to Thee.

As with joyful steps they sped
To that lowly manger bed,
There to bend the knee before
Him whom heaven and earth adore;
So may we with willing feet
Ever seek Thy mercy seat.

As they offered gifts most rare
At that manger rude and bare,
So may we with holy joy,
Pure and free from sin's alloy,
All our costliest treasures bring,
Christ, to Thee, our heavenly King.

Holy Jesus, every day
Keep us in the narrow way;
And, when earthly things are past,
Bring our ransomed souls at last
Where they need no star to guide,
Where no clouds Thy glory hide.

In the heavenly country bright
Need they no created light;
Thou its light, its joy, its crown,
Thou its sun which goes not down;
There forever may we sing
Hallelujah to our King!

In this beautifully poetic carol, William C. Dix makes mention of an important Old Testament concept. In the second stanza he talks about seeking "the mercy seat." This was the covering or lid on the ark of the covenant, the chest God instructed the ancient Israelites to construct. The ark was a sacred vessel that held the stone tablets of the testimony, a container of manna, and Aaron's rod. Its most important function, however, was in atoning for the sins of the people.

Each year on the great Day of Atonement, the high priest would enter the Holy of Holies in the tabernacle or temple. There he would sprinkle the blood, first of a bull and later of a goat, on and in front of the mercy seat. It was above this "atonement seat" that God's manifest presence dwelt. As the priest offered this yearly sacrifice before him, God had mercy on the people, forgiving their sin and rebellion.

When Christ came, he filled the roles of both high priest and sacrifice. Entering into the Holy of Holies by his own blood, he became the mediator of a new covenant, or agreement. By his blood we may now receive forgiveness and have the privilege of approaching God's throne of grace—the mercy seat.

REFLECTION

Many elements of the Old Testament tabernacle were types that pointed to Jesus. In the New Testament the book of Hebrews explores a number of these amazing symbols and prophecies, explaining how they were fulfilled by Christ. The ninth chapter in particular provides a fascinating discussion of this subject.

In that first covenant between God and Israel, there were regulations for worship and a sacred tent here on earth. There were two rooms in this tent. In the first room were a lampstand, a table, and loaves of holy bread on the table. This was called the Holy Place. Then there was a curtain, and behind the curtain was the second room called the Most Holy Place. In that room were a gold incense altar and a wooden chest called the Ark of the Covenant, which was covered with gold on all sides.

When these things were all in place, the priests went in and out of the first room regularly as they performed their religious duties. But only the high priest goes into the Most Holy Place, and only once a year, and always with blood, which he offers to God to cover his own sins and the sins the people have committed in ignorance.

This is an illustration pointing to the present time. For the gifts and sacrifices that the priests offer are not able to cleanse the consciences of the people who bring them.

So Christ has now become the High Priest over all the good things that have come. He has entered that great, perfect sanctuary in heaven, not made by human hands and not part of this created world. Once for all time he took blood into the Most Holy Place, but not the blood of goats and calves. He took his own blood, and with it he secured our salvation forever.

HEBREWS 9:1-4, 6-7, 9, 11-12

PRAYER

Jesus, thank you for becoming my high priest

and for laying down your life as a sacrifice. Thank

you for atoning for my sin once and for all. Thank

you for reconciling me to God. By your blood I

now enter the Holy of Holies to bow before the

mercy seat.

9

O LITTLE TOWN OF BETHLEHEM

PHILLIPS BROOKS, 1868

O little town of Bethlehem,
How still we see thee lie!
Above thy deep and dreamless sleep
The silent stars go by.
Yet in thy dark streets shineth
The everlasting light;
The hopes and fears of all the years
Are met in thee tonight.

For Christ is born of Mary,
And gathered all above,
While mortals sleep, the angels keep
Their watch of wond'ring love.

O morning stars, together
Proclaim the holy birth,
And praises sing to God the King,
And peace to men on earth.

How silently, how silently
The wondrous gift is given!
So God imparts to human hearts
The blessings of His heaven.
No ear may hear His coming,
But in this world of sin,
Where meek souls will receive Him, still
The dear Christ enters in.

O holy Child of Bethlehem!
Descend to us, we pray;
Cast out our sin, and enter in,
Be born in us today.
We hear the Christmas angels
The great glad tidings tell;
O come to us, abide with us,
Our Lord Emmanuel!

While touring the Holy Land in 1865, Phillips Brooks spent Christmas Eve in and around Bethlehem, looking out over the shepherds' fields, gazing at the town, and attending a church service. What he saw there captured his imagination. "It seemed as if I could hear voices I know well," he said, "telling each other of the 'Wonderful Night' of the Saviour's birth." Three years later he poured his impressions of that night into this song.

Brooks was awed by the magnitude of the "wondrous gift" that had been given. On the first Christmas, God presented mankind with a bundle of life. Wrapped up in swaddling clothes in that crude stable in Bethlehem was his own Son. As this carol puts it, his divine intention was to "impart to human hearts the blessings of His heaven." Jesus' birth was just the start of that plan. The gift found his ultimate fulfillment on a cross at Calvary some thirty-three years later. The death and resurrection of Christ made God's blessing—forgiveness and eternal life with him—available to all.

REFLECTION

Thanksgiving is an appropriate attitude to adopt at
Christmas. Let these verses help you present a
sacrifice of thanksgiving to the Father and invite
the Son to make his home in you.

*He was handed over to die because of our sins, and he was raised
from the dead to make us right with God. Therefore, since we
have been made right in God's sight by faith, we have peace with
God because of what Jesus Christ our Lord has done for us.
Because of our faith, Christ has brought us into this place of
highest privilege where we now stand, and we confidently and
joyfully look forward to sharing God's glory.*

ROMANS 4:25–5:2

*Now there is no condemnation for those who belong to Christ
Jesus. For the power of the life-giving Spirit has freed you
through Christ Jesus from the power of sin that leads to death.*

ROMANS 8:1-2

Thank God for his Son—a gift too wonderful for words!

2 CORINTHIANS 9:15

PRAYER

I give thanks, Father, for your indescribable gift. How amazing is the love that compelled you to send your Son that I might have life! I welcome you, Jesus. Show me my sin that I may be free from it, and that your home—my heart—may be pure and holy. O come to me, abide in me, my Lord Emmanuel.

10

O Thou Joyful Day

Traditional German
Anonymous, Eighteenth Century

O thou joyful day, O thou blessed day,
Holy, peaceful Christmastide!
Earth's hopes awaken, Christ life has taken,
Laud Him, O laud Him on every side!

O thou joyful day, O thou blessed day,
Holy, peaceful Christmastide!
Christ's light is beaming, our souls redeeming,
Laud Him, O laud Him on every side!

O thou joyful day, O thou blessed day,
Holy, peaceful Christmastide!
King of all glory, we bow before Thee,
Laud Him, O laud Him on every side!

The hope which was awakened at the Incarnation went far beyond humankind. Adam's sin had subjected the entire universe to death and decay. Paul tells us that man's fall frustrated creation, forcing it to endure a painful period of waiting until it could be redeemed and liberated from bondage. The holiday we call Christmas is a celebration of that Redeemer's birth.

Paul further explains that creation is today eagerly awaiting the revelation of the sons of God. The Creator's handiwork is actually groaning in anticipation of the day when our true identity as the redeemed children of God is made known. When Jesus returns and that disclosure is made, all of nature—the heavens, the stars, the earth, the sea, the fields, mountains, hills, trees, and rivers—will shout and sing for joy.

The light of hope which was ignited on that first Christmas continues to burn brightly as God's people and his handiwork look forward to Jesus' return.

REFLECTION

To redeem means to buy back or recover. God
sent Jesus to buy back that which was God's in
the first place. Rather than give us up for lost,
God paid a heavy price—the lifeblood of his only
Son—to rescue us and restore us to a relationship
with him. As you look up the following selec-
tions, thank God for his willingness to pay such a
cost for your life.

*Christ has rescued us from the curse pronounced by the law.
When he was hung on the cross, he took upon himself the curse
for our wrongdoing. For it is written in the Scriptures, "Cursed
is everyone who is hung on a tree." Through the work of Christ
Jesus, God has blessed the Gentiles with the same blessing he
promised to Abraham, and we Christians receive the promised
Holy Spirit through faith.*

GALATIANS 3:13-14

*He is so rich in kindness that he purchased our freedom through
the blood of his Son, and our sins are forgiven. He has showered
his kindness on us, along with all wisdom and understanding.*

EPHESIANS 1:7-8

That is why he is the one who mediates the new covenant between God and people, so that all who are invited can receive the eternal inheritance God has promised them. For Christ died to set them free from the penalty of the sins they had committed under that first covenant.

HEBREWS 9:15

Give thanks to the Lord, for he is good! His faithful love endures forever. Has the Lord redeemed you? Then speak out! Tell others he has saved you from your enemies. For he has gathered the exiles from many lands, from east and west, from north and south.

PSALM 107:1-3

PRAYER

Father, thank you for purchasing my life with the blood of your Son. My mind can hardly comprehend such love. I am forever grateful. Like the carol writer, I too bow down before the King of *all glory. Jesus, Lamb of God, you are worthy to*

be lauded—praised and extolled. Thank you for

enduring the shame, anguish, and torture of the

cross to rescue me from death. From this day forth

through all eternity I will lift glory and honor to

your name.

11

THE HAPPY CHRISTMAS COMES ONCE MORE

NICOLAI F. S. GRUNDTRIG, 1817

The happy Christmas comes once more,
The heavenly Guest is at the door,
The blessed words the shepherds thrill,
The joyous tidings: Peace, good will.

O wake, our hearts, in gladness sing,
And keep our Christmas with our King,
Like the sound of mighty water rolls.

Come, Jesus, glorious heavenly Guest,
Keep Thine own Christmas in our breast;
Then David's harpstrings, hushed so long,
Shall swell our jubilee of song.

What is Christmas? Is it simply a yearly excuse to engage in extended spending frenzies? Is it nothing more than an annual exercise in overindulgence? Is the holiday season merely a chance to cut loose and party? While Christians are quick to answer these questions with a resounding "no," we too often miss the real "reason for the season."

Christmas is more than just a day set aside to mark the birth of an ancient religious leader. It does commemorate Christ's birth, but it also has a much greater, more practical significance. In Christmas we find a unique opportunity to celebrate a two-thousand-year-old birth with the birthday boy himself. The message of Christmas is that Jesus is alive to celebrate with us. As this carol reminds us, he is the guest of honor at this wondrous yearly feast. He is the star attraction and central focus around which all the festivities should revolve. Even now Jesus is patiently waiting to gain entry to our hearts, homes, churches, and cities, so that he may celebrate this joyous occasion with us.

REFLECTION

In the flurry of activity that we call Christmas, our
attention is easily distracted from the one we seek
to honor. Yet the heavenly Guest continues to call
to us. He patiently raps on the door of our heart,
ready to come in and fellowship with us. What
will our response be? Will we hear him? Will we
welcome him in?

*Look! Here I stand at the door and knock. If you hear
me calling and open the door, I will come in,
and we will share a meal as friends.*

REVELATION 3:20

PRAYER

Lord, I hear you knocking. Come in and make

your home in my heart. Dwell here with me, so

that my body may be your house, your temple.

Cause living song to rise from my soul as I keep

this Christmas with you, my loving King.

12

O HOLY NIGHT!

M. CAPPEAU DE ROQUEMAURE
TRANSLATED BY JOHN S. DWIGHT, NINETEENTH CENTURY

O holy night! The stars are brightly shining,
It is the night of the dear Savior's birth;
Long lay the world in sin and error pining,
Till He appeared and the soul felt its worth.
A thrill of hope, the weary world rejoices,
For yonder breaks a new and glorious morn;
Fall on your knees,
Oh, hear the angel voices!
O night divine,
O night when Christ was born!
O night, O holy night, O night divine!

Led by the light of faith serenely beaming,
With glowing hearts by His cradle we stand;
So led by light of a star sweetly gleaming,
Here came the Wise Men from Orient land.
The King of kings lay thus in lowly manger,
In all our trials born to be our friend;
He knows our need,
To our weakness is no stranger;
Behold your King,
Before Him lowly bend!

Truly He taught us to love one another;
His law is love, and His gospel is peace.
Chains shall he break, for the slave is our brother,
And in His name all oppression shall cease.
Sweet hymns of joy in grateful chorus raise we,
Let all within us praise His holy name!
Christ is the Lord! O praise His name forever!
His power and glory evermore proclaim!

This French carol is a lyrical retelling of the Good News of the gospel message. In the first stanza De Roquemaure asks us to close our eyes and imagine the world before the advent of Jesus. There it lay, "in sin and error pining." To appreciate the truthfulness of this phrase we must understand that the word *pining* means the wasting away of the human spirit as it grieves, mourns, and endures pain. This desperate state was the result of the Fall—Adam and Eve's disobedience in the Garden. Banished from God's presence, the human race was left to be tormented by sin until . . . "He appeared." Suddenly there was cause for hope, suddenly there was cause for joy.

In the next stanza the writer expounds on the Incarnation—the divine walking in human form. Rather than judge from above, the Lord came down and experienced our need and weakness firsthand. He now truly understands our situation and offers us the necessary comfort and grace to deal with it. Furthermore, De Roquemaure explains, this Jesus welcomes us as friends. Mere humans becoming friends with God? It's mind-boggling. No wonder the hearts of those who beheld this child glowed.

Messiah's mission is the focus of the final stanza. Love is the law of the kingdom he came to establish in our hearts. Mercy and justice are its outworkings—freedom and celebration, its rewards. De Roquemaure leaves us with a familiar exhortation, the command that sounds throughout God's kingdom: "Praise His name forever! His power and glory evermore proclaim!"

REFLECTION

The gospel message, though infinitely profound, can be summed up in three simple parts: Jesus came, Jesus died, Jesus rose again. He came to save us, died to free us, and rose victorious to rule over us. Scripture makes it clear that he is to be our Savior, Redeemer, and King. Ask him to reveal himself in these roles as you read the following verses.

Now we believe because we have heard him ourselves, not just because of what you told us. He is indeed the Savior of the world.

JOHN 4:42

Praise the Lord, the God of Israel, because he has visited his people and redeemed them.

When the right time came, God sent his Son, born of a woman, subject to the law. God sent him to buy freedom for us who were slaves to the law, so that he could adopt us as his very own children.

LUKE 1:68; GALATIANS 4:4-5

As they reached the place where the road started down from the Mount of Olives, all of his followers began to shout and sing as they walked along, praising God for all the wonderful miracles they had seen. "Bless the King who comes in the name of the Lord!"

On his robe and thigh was written this title: King of kings and Lord of lords.

LUKE 19:37-38; REVELATION 19:16

PRAYER

Thank you, Jesus, for securing my salvation and

freedom. Thank you for loving me so much that

you came to rescue me. I testify that you are my

Savior. As I am washed by your blood, bathed in

blessed forgiveness, I confess that you are my Re-

deemer. In gratitude I fall on my knees and sub-

mit to your rule and reign. I exalt you as my King.

I will praise you forever. Your power and glory I

will evermore proclaim.

THOU DIDST LEAVE THY THRONE

EMILY E. S. ELLIOT, 1864

Thou didst leave Thy throne and Thy kingly crown
When Thou camest to earth for me;
But in Bethlehem's home there was found no room
For Thy holy nativity.
O come to my heart, Lord Jesus—
There is room in my heart for Thee!

Heaven's arches rang when the angels sang,
Proclaiming Thy royal decree;
But in lowly birth didst Thou come to earth,
And in great humility.

The foxes found rest, and the birds their nest
In the shade of a forest tree;
But Thy couch was the sod, O Thou Son of God,
In the deserts of Galilee.

Thou camest, O Lord, with the living Word
That should set Thy people free;
But with mocking scorn and with crown of thorn
They bore Thee to Calvary.

When the heavens shall ring and the angels sing
At Thy coming to victory,
Let Thy voice call me home, saying, "Yet there is room,
There is room at My side for thee!"
And my heart shall rejoice, Lord Jesus,
When Thou comest and callest for me.

Jesus' lowly birth foretold of a lowly life to come. "The foxes found rest, and the birds their nest," Elliot says, paraphrasing Matthew 8:20, "but Thy couch was the sod, O Thou Son of God." He not only had nowhere to lay his head but was scorned and rejected by the very creatures he had come to liberate. Still, he willingly subjected himself to their cruel torture and allowed himself to be executed in order to win their freedom.

Have you ever wondered why Jesus agreed to endure such shame and pain? Why did he leave his throne and his kingly crown to come to earth? What could have possibly motivated the Son of God to become a man? The answer is profound, yet simple: love. The Father's love for us is so great, so very intense, that it motivated him to go to whatever lengths necessary to draw us to his side—even asking his own Son to discard his glory, enter creation, and give up his life. And Jesus, out of his love for the Father and his love for us, said yes. What a wonderful testimony to the size and scope of God's unfailing, unmerited love.

REFLECTION

Read the following passages carefully. They are very familiar to many of us, perhaps too familiar. Look them up in various translations. Ask the Lord

to take these verses off the page and apply them
to your heart.

For God so loved the world that he gave his only Son,
so that everyone who believes in him will not perish
but have eternal life. God did not send his Son into the world
to condemn it, but to save it.

May your roots go down deep into the soil of God's marvelous
love. And may you have the power to understand, as all God's
people should, how wide, how long, how high, and how deep his
love really is. May you experience the love of Christ, though it is
so great you will never fully understand it. Then you will be
filled with the fullness of life and power that comes from God.

I am convinced that nothing can ever separate us from his love.
Death can't, and life can't. The angels can't, and the demons
can't. Our fears for today, our worries about tomorrow, and even
the powers of hell can't keep God's love away. Whether we are
high above the sky or in the deepest ocean, nothing in all creation

will ever be able to separate us from the love of God that is revealed in Christ Jesus our Lord.

ROMANS 8:38-39

PRAYER

O come to my heart, Lord Jesus. There is room in my heart for Thee. At Thy coming victory let Thy voice call me home, saying, "Yet there is room, there is room at My side for thee!" And my heart shall rejoice, Lord Jesus, when Thou comest and callest for me.

ANGELS, FROM THE REALMS OF GLORY

JAMES MONTGOMERY, 1816

Angels, from the realms of glory,
Wing your flight o'er all the earth;
Ye who sang creation's story,
Now proclaim Messiah's birth:

Come and worship, come and worship,
Worship Christ, the newborn King.

Shepherds, in the field abiding,
Watching o'er your flocks by night,
God with man is now residing,
Yonder shines the infant Light:

Sages, leave your contemplations,
Brighter visions beam afar;
Seek the great Desire of nations,
Ye have seen His natal star.

Some say that Moravian hymn writer James Montgomery, who penned more than four hundred songs, rivaled Charles Wesley and Isaac Watts in skill. This, his best known work, has been heralded as a masterpiece. One observer even argued that "for comprehensiveness, appropriateness of expression, force and elevation of sentiment, it may challenge comparison with any hymn that was ever written, in any language or country." While that may or may not be true, it has certainly become a holiday favorite.

Though much could be said for the content of the descriptive lyrics, the simple refrain clearly reflects the essence of the Christmas message. The invitation to worship, which was accorded the angels, shepherds, and sages, continues to issue forth. This call is as urgent and open today as it was two thousand years ago. No longer a "newborn," the risen Christ is all the more worthy of our praise. What an honor we have—the privilege of bowing down before the King of kings!

REFLECTION

Let these verses lead you into his presence so that you may know and experience the joy and delight of worship.

Give honor to the Lord, you angels; give honor to the Lord for his glory and strength. Give honor to the Lord for the glory of his name. Worship the Lord in the splendor of his holiness.

PSALM 29:1-2

Because of your unfailing love, I can enter your house; with deepest awe I will worship at your Temple.

PSALM 5:7

Shout joyful praises to God, all the earth! Sing about the glory of his name! Tell the world how glorious he is. Say to God, "How awesome are your deeds! Your enemies cringe before your mighty power. Everything on earth will worship you; they will sing your praises, shouting your name in glorious songs."

PSALM 66:1-4

PRAYER

I humble myself before your awesome presence, O Lord. Search my heart that it may be pure before you. My desire this day is to respond to the call that sounds from your holy throne, the invitation which forever resonates through all heaven and earth. I bow before you, Living God. I come that I might worship Jesus.

15

GOLDEN MORNINGS

ENGLISH TRADITIONAL, EIGHTEENTH CENTURY

They saw the light shine out afar
On Christmas in the morning;
And straight they knew it was the star,
That came to give them warning:
Then did they fall on bended knee,
The light their heads adorning,
And praised the Lord, who let them see
His glory in the morning.

For three short years he went abroad
And set men's hearts a-burning;
That mission turned the world to God
And brought the night to morning:

He bore for man repulse and pain,
Ingratitude and scorning;
He suffered, died, and rose again
At Easter in the morning.

O every thought be of his grace,
On each day in the morning;
And for his kingdom's loveliness
Our souls be ever yearning:
So may we live, to Heaven our hearts
In hope forever turning;
Then may we die, as each departs,
In joy at our new morning.

The three stanzas of this carol encompass the whole of the Christian life: Christmas, Easter, and the walk of faith. Jesus came, and light shattered the darkness. Jesus died and rose again, and hope sprang up afresh. Jesus invites us to come, and his grace seeks us out. This melodic capsule of Good News is what the world is dying to hear.

Although the song has much to offer, one particular

phrase seems to stand out. The writer says that during the days of his earthly ministry, Jesus "set men's hearts a-burning." This is true in at least two distinct ways. First, Jesus fanned to flame the hunger for God that resides in each person's heart. By becoming a mediator between humans and God, he renewed the hope that had nearly died in the breasts of humankind—that they could know God. He ignited a host of hearts to seek the Father.

Jesus is also described in Scripture as a refiner's fire—an extremely hot flame that burns away the dross and impurities found in gold and silver. He not only came to set hearts afire but to confront, root out, and defeat sin in all of its various forms. Even those men who resisted his mission must have felt the heat of that fiery message as it burned deep within them.

REFLECTION

Whether it be a searing hunger for God or a flaming consciousness of sin, each encounter with Jesus leaves our hearts burning. As you read the

following verses, ask the Lord to purify your heart
and engulf you in his fiery passion.

The Lord your God is a devouring fire, a jealous God.

DEUTERONOMY 4:24

Who will be able to endure it when he comes? Who will be able to
stand and face him when he appears? For he will be like a blazing
fire that refines metal or like a strong soap that whitens clothes.
He will sit and judge like a refiner of silver, watching closely as
the dross is burned away.

MALACHI 3:2-3

I baptize with water those who turn from their sins and turn to
God. But someone is coming soon who is far greater than I
am—so much greater that I am not even worthy to be his slave.
He will baptize you with the Holy Spirit and with fire.

MATTHEW 3:11

PRAYER

All-consuming Fire, I humbly submit myself to the testing of your mighty hand. Burn away all that is not holy, all that is not of you. Refiner's Fire, separate the dross that weighs down my heart, the evil and sin that cannot bear the brilliance of your presence. Place in me your fire—a zeal for you, for your kingdom, and for the lost whom you long to embrace. Amen.

16

GOOD KING WENCESLAS

JOHN M. NEALE, 1853

Good King Wenceslas looked out, on the Feast of Stephen,
When the snow lay round about, deep and crisp and even:
Brightly shone the moon that night,
though the frost was cruel,
When a poor man came in sight, gathering winter fuel.

"Hither, page, and stand by me, if thou know'st it, telling,
Yonder peasant, who is he? where and what his dwelling?"
"Sire, he lives a good league hence,
underneath the mountain,
Right against the forest fence, by Saint Agnes' fountain."

"Bring me flesh, and bring me wine,
bring me pinelogs hither;
Thou and I will see him dine, when we bear them thither."
Page and monarch, forth they went,
forth they went together;
Through the rude wind's wild lament
and the bitter weather.

"Sire, the night is darker now,
and the wind blows stronger;
Fails my heart, I know not how; I can go no longer."
"Mark my footsteps, good my page;
tread thou in them boldly:
Thou shalt find the winter's rage
freeze thy blood less coldly."

In his master's steps he trod, where the snow lay dinted;
Heat was in the very sod, which the Saint had printed.
Therefore, Christian men, be sure,
wealth or rank possessing,
Ye who now will bless the poor,
shall yourselves find blessing.

Though this carol does not mention Christ by name or recount his birth, it contains the essence of the Christmas message: God reaching out to humanity.

King Wenceslas the Holy, who ruled Bohemia from A.D. 1378 to 1419, was known for his good works and his care of the poor. In this song, which is based on legend, John Neale portrays him as a man of grace. Rather than order his servants to leave a few morsels or fire logs for the underprivileged peasant or send his page out to find the man and deliver some seasonal gift, Wenceslas chooses to take action himself. Leaving the warmth of his castle, the king braves fierce wind and bitter cold to search out the man. Whether factual or myth, Wenceslas's great compassion in this song reflects God's heart for the lost and the poor.

Jesus said that he came to seek and to save the lost. This is the primary reason that God chose to become man. Not content to send others in his place, the King of glory left heaven and came looking for us. Braving hostile elements, even unto death, he personally sought us out.

To those who have been found, who have been rescued and now reside safe and secure within the walls
of his kingdom, he gives this charge: "Follow me." Like
the page, we are to follow in our Master's footsteps as
he continues to pursue the abandoned, the orphaned,
the poor, and the lost. We shall undoubtedly encounter
darkness and the bitter winds of trial and testing as we
submit to such service. Yet he goes before us, clearing
the path, shielding us from the wind, and leading us
forward. As we boldly tread in Jesus' steps, we find
ourselves revived by his strength, revitalized by his
power, and warmed by his holy fire.

REFLECTION

We shall find blessing as we minister to the poor.
The following verses illustrate God's fervent
desire to reach out to those in need.

*It is sin to despise one's neighbors; blessed are those who help the
poor. Those who oppress the poor insult their Maker, but those
who help the poor honor him.*

PROVERBS 14:21, 31

Pure and lasting religion in the sight of God our Father means that we must care for orphans and widows in their troubles, and refuse to let the world corrupt us.

JAMES 1:27

When the Son of Man comes in his glory, and all the angels with him, then he will sit upon his glorious throne. All the nations will be gathered in his presence, and he will separate them as a shepherd separates the sheep from the goats. He will place the sheep at his right hand and the goats at his left. Then the King will say to those on the right, "Come, you who are blessed by my Father, inherit the Kingdom prepared for you from the foundation of the world. For I was hungry, and you fed me.
I was thirsty, and you gave me a drink. I was a stranger, and you invited me into your home. I was naked, and you gave me clothing.
I was sick, and you cared for me. I was in prison, and you visited me."

Then these righteous ones will reply, "Lord, when did we ever see you hungry and feed you? Or thirsty and give you something to drink? Or a stranger and show you hospitality? Or naked and give you clothing? When did we ever see you sick or in prison, and visit you?" And the King will tell them, "I assure you, when you did it to one of the least of these my brothers and sisters, you were doing it to me!"

MATTHEW 25:31-40

PRAYER

Ask God to bring you into contact with those who are spiritually and physically needy, at Christmas and throughout the year. Allow him to show you how to minister to them and let him provide you with the resources. Tell him that you want to be a faithful servant, walking in the Master's steps and extending his blessing to the poor and lost.

17

LOVE CAME DOWN AT CHRISTMAS

CHRISTINA ROSSETTI, 1893

Love came down at Christmas,
Love all lovely, Love divine;
Love was born at Christmas,
Stars and angels gave the sign.

Worship we the Godhead,
Love incarnate, Love divine;
Worship we our Jesus:
But wherewith for sacred sign?

Love shall be our token,
Love be yours and love be mine,
Love to God and all men,
Love for plea and gift and sign.

This carol is a poetic paraphrase of a theme that runs throughout the first epistle of John. The apostle says that God is love, that his very nature and character are summed up in that one word. John goes on to explain that God displayed his love by sending his only Son into the world to atone for our sin. As Rossetti puts it, he is "love incarnate, love divine." In the popular vernacular, Jesus is "love with legs."

John further notes that Jesus is an expression of the highest form of love in that he laid down his own life for his friends. By enduring shame and suffering, he became a living portrait of God's love. Contemporary songwriter Graham Kendrick marveled at this: "My Lord, what love is this, that pays so dearly . . .? Amazing love, O what sacrifice, the Son of God, giv'n for me. My debt he pays, and my death he dies, that I might live."

John, Rossetti, and Kendrick were all astounded by the extent, abundance, and generosity of God's love. Yet even as they reveled in it, they recognized that it demanded a response. It was meant to be received and lived. As Rossetti reminds us, "Love shall be our token." Encountering the living Christ brings us face-to-face with pure love. This experience transforms us into a people who are characterized by love. The love of God becomes the token or evidence of our identity, the sign by which others may recognize us as followers of Jesus.

REFLECTION

John mentions love often in his writing. Read the Gospel of John and look for the word love. The following verses will provide you with a brief overview.

For God so loved the world that he gave his only Son, so that everyone who believes in him will not perish but have eternal life.

JOHN 3:16

Now I am giving you a new commandment: Love each other. Just as I have loved you, you should love each other. Your love for one another will prove to the world that you are my disciples.

JOHN 13:34-35

I have loved you even as the Father has loved me. Remain in my love. When you obey me, you remain in my love, just as I obey my Father and remain in his love.

JOHN 15:9-10

We know what real love is because Christ gave up his life for us. And so we also ought to give up our lives for our Christian brothers and sisters. But if anyone has enough money to live well and sees a brother or sister in need and refuses to help—how can God's love be in that person? Dear children, let us stop just saying we love each other; let us really show it by our actions.

1 JOHN 3:16-18

Dear friends, let us continue to love one another, for love comes from God. Anyone who loves is born of God and knows God. But anyone who does not love does not know God—for God is love.

1 JOHN 4:7-8

PRAYER

Father, in celebrating Christmas I am celebrating Jesus, the expression of your lavish, amazing, divine love. At the carol's urging, I worship him, love incarnate. May the love of Christ flow like rivers from the depths of my being. May I henceforth be known as a lover of God and of men. As I choose to walk with you this day, let love be the token of my life.

18

I HEARD THE BELLS ON CHRISTMAS DAY

HENRY W. LONGFELLOW, 1863

I heard the bells on Christmas day
Their old familiar carols play,
And wild and sweet
The words repeat
Of peace on earth, good will to men!

I thought how, as the day had come,
The belfries of all Christendom
Had rolled along
The unbroken song
Of peace on earth, good will to men!

And in despair I bowed my head:
"There is no peace on earth," I said,

"For hate is strong
And mocks the song
Of peace on earth, good will to men!"

Then pealed the bells more loud and deep:
"God is not dead; nor doth he sleep!
The wrong shall fail,
The right prevail,
With peace on earth, good will to men!"

Henry Wadsworth Longfellow wrote the words of this familiar carol during a period of intense conflict. The nation was locked in a bloody battle, North pitted against South in a struggle to the death, as the Civil War threatened to tear the United States apart.

Surveying the situation, Longfellow was overcome with despair. It appeared that evil had triumphed over good, strife had replaced peace. The message of Christmas seemed distant, even futile. Then he heard it—the sound of the bells. Church bells ringing, proclaiming peace on earth, good will to men. Surrounded on all sides by death and hatred, the bells were a necessary reminder that God was at work. He had not forsaken his people.

Just as the bells encouraged Longfellow, the words of this carol refresh and renew our hope. They remind us that no matter what happens, no matter how bleak the circumstance, God is still in control and he is faithful. "Jesus is alive!" the bells continue to ring out. "And his kingdom will never end!"

REFLECTION

Is God faithful? Does he really mean what he says? Can we trust him? The answer is yes. Let these promises enliven your faith and give you the confidence to stand firm against trials and tribulations.

Understand, therefore, that the Lord your God is indeed God. He is the faithful God who keeps his covenant for a thousand generations and constantly loves those who love him and obey his commands.

DEUTERONOMY 7:9

The Lord helps the fallen and lifts up those bent beneath their loads. All eyes look to you for help; you give them their food as they need it. When you open your hand, you satisfy the hunger and thirst of every living thing. The Lord is righteous in everything he does; he is filled with kindness. The Lord is close to all those who call on him, yes, to all who call on him sincerely. He fulfills the desires of those who fear him; he hears their cries for help and rescues them. The Lord protects all those who love him.

PSALM 145:14-20

God will surely do this for you, for he always does just what he says, and he is the one who invited you into this wonderful friendship with his Son, Jesus Christ our Lord.

1 CORINTHIANS 1:9

I look up to the mountains—does my help come from there? My help comes from the Lord, who made the heavens and the earth! He will not let you stumble and fall; the one who watches over you will not sleep. Indeed, he who watches over Israel never tires and never sleeps. The Lord himself watches over you! The Lord stands beside you as your protective shade. The sun will not hurt you by day, nor the moon at night. The Lord keeps you from all

evil and preserves your life. The Lord keeps watch over you as
you come and go, both now and forever.

PSALM 121

PRAYER

Though this world grows dark and desperate, I
will not lose hope. My hope and trust are in you,
the almighty, ever living God. May the truth and
reality of your power and faithfulness ever ring
afresh in my heart.

19

THE FIRST NOWELL

ENGLISH TRADITIONAL, SEVENTEENTH CENTURY

The first Nowell the angel did say
Was to certain poor shepherds in fields as they lay;
In fields where they lay keeping their sheep
On a cold winter's night that was so deep.

Nowell, Nowell, Nowell, Nowell,
Born is the King of Israel!

They looked up and saw a star
Shining in the east beyond them far,
And to the earth it gave great light,
And so it continued both day and night.

And by the light of that same star,
Three wise men came from country far;

To seek for a king was their intent
And to follow the star wherever it went.

This star drew nigh to the northwest;
O'er Bethlehem it took its rest,
And there it did both stop and stay,
Right over the place where Jesus lay.

Then entered in those wise men three
Full reverently upon their knee,
And offered there in his presence
Their gold, and myrrh, and frankincense.

Then let us all with one accord
Sing praises to our heavenly Lord;
That hath made heaven and earth of naught
And with his blood mankind hath bought.

Everyone has heard the word *nowell* (or *noel* as it is now commonly spelled) in carols, seen it on store windows, and found it adorning Christmas cards. It has become such an overused term that we risk forgetting just what it means. Here the carolist holds up his hand. "Stop!" he seems to shout. "Time out! Pause and consider what this noel business is all about."

The word *noel* literally means "birth." Amidst the simple story, the writer explains that the noel the angels were so excited about was that of the King of Israel.

Noel has also come to be synonymous with Christmas and Christmas carols (even according to the dictionary). This song really deals with all three meanings: the birth of Christ, the advent of his coming, and the music associated with it. As we celebrate the wondrous events surrounding the first noel, the writer points to its significance and calls us to lift up a new noel, to sing together a song of praise to the one who has purchased us with his blood.

REFLECTION

Music is an important way for us to express praise and worship to God. It was instituted by him before the creation of the earth and is referred to some 839 times in the Bible. The Psalms, for instance, continually exhort us to "praise the Lord in song." As you read the following verses, ask the Lord to give you a new song (noel) with which to honor him.

Let the godly sing with joy to the Lord, for it is fitting to praise him. Praise the Lord with melodies on the lyre; make music for him on the ten-stringed harp. Sing new songs of praise to him; play skillfully on the harp and sing with joy.

PSALM 33:1-3

He has given me a new song to sing, a hymn of praise to our God. Many will see what he has done and be astounded. They will put their trust in the Lord.

PSALM 40:3

Sing a new song to the Lord! Let the whole earth sing to the Lord! Sing to the Lord; bless his name. Each day proclaim the good news that he saves.

PSALM 96:1-2

Sing psalms and hymns and spiritual songs among yourselves, making music to the Lord in your hearts. . . . Always give thanks for everything to God the Father in the name of our Lord Jesus Christ.

EPHESIANS 5:19-20

PRAYER

Hear, O Lord, the song of praise that rises from the depths of my being. It wells up from the joy in my heart and flows like a fountain, bubbling up over my lips. Receive this song as a token of my love, a sign of my admiration for you. May it be pleasing to your ears. May it bring a smile to your glorious face.

O Little One

SAMUEL SCHEIDT, 1650

O Little One sweet, O Little One mild,
Thy Father's purpose thou hast fulfilled;
Thou cam'st from heaven to mortal ken,
Equal to be with us poor men.

O Little One sweet, O Little One mild,
With joy thou hast the whole world filled;
Thou comest here from heaven's domain,
To bring men comfort in their pain.

O Little One sweet, O Little One mild,
In thee Love's beauties are all distilled;
Then light in us thy love's bright flame,
That we may give thee back the same.

O Little One sweet, O Little One mild,
Help us to do as thou hast willed.
Lo, all we have belongs to thee!
Ah, keep us in our fealty!

What contrasts this carol brings to light! In each stanza it rightly deems Jesus the sweet mild babe yet tells of the incredible feats he accomplished as a man. On that first Christmas morning, who could have foreseen all that the tiny child in the manger would eventually fulfill? The author explains that Jesus faithfully served the Father's sovereign plan. He filled the world with joy and comforted those who were suffering under great affliction by bringing heaven down to earth.

Jesus came to proclaim and demonstrate the kingdom of God. Wherever he went he preached the Good News and freed those in bondage. He asks us to do the same, fulfilling the Father's purpose. We are to be his hands, reaching out to those in need. We are to be his feet, seeking out those who are lonely and afraid. We are to be his mouth, speaking God's message of love to those who so desperately need to hear it.

If we hope to attain to such a high calling, we must call out to Jesus. Only by his grace and power will we ever remain faithful to that precious duty (fealty). As we listen to his call to action and look to the broken, hurting world, we can only cry out with the carol writer, "Ah, keep us in our fealty!"

REFLECTION

Jesus' ministry didn't end with his ascension into heaven. It continues today through everyone in whom the Spirit of God dwells. As you consider the passages listed below, petition the Lord for a greater revelation of the calling he has placed upon your life.

The Spirit of the Lord is upon me, for he has appointed me to preach Good News to the poor. He has sent me to proclaim that captives will be released, that the blind will see, that the downtrodden will be freed from their oppressors, and that the time of the Lord's favor has come.

LUKE 4:18-19

The truth is, anyone who believes in me will do the same works
I have done, and even greater works, because
I am going to be with the Father.

JOHN 14:12

These signs will accompany those who believe: They will cast out
demons in my name, and they will speak new languages. They
will be able to handle snakes with safety, and if they drink
anything poisonous, it won't hurt them. They will be able to
place their hands on the sick and heal them.

MARK 16:17-18

PRAYER

Jesus, impart to me the bright flame of your love,

that I may function as your humble servant. Fill

me with your Spirit, that I may attend to those in

need. May your life so flow through me that your

ministry would be displayed in my feeble hands,

112

feet, and mouth. May you receive the glory as I

go forth in response to your call to touch the lost,

the poor, the sick, and the dying.

21

FROM HEAVEN ABOVE

MARTIN LUTHER, 1535

From heaven above to earth I come
To bear good news to every home;
Glad tidings of great joy I bring,
Whereof I now will say and sing:

"To you this night is born a Child
Of Mary, chosen mother mild;
This little Child of lowly birth
Shall be the joy of all the earth.

"'Tis Christ, our God, who far on high
Hath heard your sad and bitter cry;
Himself will your salvation be,
Himself from sin will make you free."

Welcome to earth, Thou noble guest,
Through whom e'en wicked men are blest!
Thou comest to share our misery;
What can we render, Lord, to Thee?

Ah, dearest Jesus, Holy Child,
Make Thee a bed, soft, undefiled,
Within my heart that it may be
A quiet chamber kept for Thee!

Glory to God in highest heaven,
Who unto men His Son hath given,
While angels sing with pious mirth
A glad new year to all the earth.

We often wonder how we can please God. What can we do to satisfy him? Spend more time in prayer? Study the Bible more often? Attend more church functions? While there is nothing wrong with these activities, they miss the point. God isn't interested in our performance.

In this carol Luther reminds us of God's true priorities, those things which bring him pleasure. First, he is delighted when we believe in Jesus. "Himself will your salvation be, Himself from sin will make you free." By acknowledging those truths, we make the Father happy.

After choosing to believe in his Son, the Lord asks us to receive him. Jesus is more than just a historical fact. Because he rose from the dead and lives today, he is a present reality, someone to know and be known by. When we welcome his Son into our life, it gives the Father great satisfaction.

God is jealous for our hearts. That is what he has been after all along. In sending Jesus he set about wooing us, drawing us by his love in hopes of gaining our hearts. When our "quiet chamber" becomes his possession and he is allowed to take up residence there, he is well pleased.

Finally, after turning our hearts over to God, we are released to worship him. Our praise arises out of love for him rather than religious bondage. We can then rejoice with Luther in singing "Glory to God in highest heaven, Who unto men His Son hath given."

REFLECTION

Serving God out of love rather than performing for or earning his approval is an ongoing challenge. Each day we must examine our hearts to determine our motivations. Are we becoming like the Pharisees, bound by laws but distant from God? Ask the Lord to reveal your heart as you read his Word.

The Lord says, "These people say they are mine.
They honor me with their lips, but their hearts are far away.
And their worship of me amounts to nothing more than
human laws learned by rote."

ISAIAH 29:13

No one can ever be made right in God's sight by doing what his law commands. For the more we know God's law, the clearer it becomes that we aren't obeying it.

ROMANS 3:20

God has shown us a different way of being right in his sight—not by obeying the law but by the way promised in the Scriptures long ago. We are made right in God's sight when we trust in

118

*Jesus Christ to take away our sins. And we all can be saved
in this same way, no matter who we are or what we have done.
For all have sinned; all fall short of God's glorious standard.
Yet now God in his gracious kindness declares us not guilty.
He has done this through Christ Jesus, who has freed us by
taking away our sins.*

ROMANS 3:21-24

*God saved you by his special favor when you believed. And you
can't take credit for this; it is a gift from God.*

EPHESIANS 2:8

*With Jesus' help, let us continually offer our sacrifice of praise to
God by proclaiming the glory of his name.*

HEBREWS 13:15

PRAYER

*F*ather, my one desire is to please you. To that end I welcome your Son, Jesus, into my heart, so that it may ever be your possession. Come, Lord, take your rest in the quiet chamber I have kept for you.

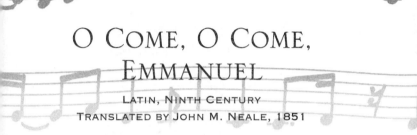

22

O COME, O COME, EMMANUEL

LATIN, NINTH CENTURY
TRANSLATED BY JOHN M. NEALE, 1851

O come, O come, Emmanuel,
And ransom captive Israel,
That mourns in lonely exile here
Until the Son of God appear.

Rejoice, rejoice! Emmanuel
Shall come to thee, O Israel.

O come, o come, Thou Lord of Might,
Who to Thy tribes on Sinai's height
In ancient times didst give the law
In cloud, and majesty, and awe.

O come, Thou Rod of Jesse, free
Thine own from Satan's tyranny;
From depths of hell Thy people save
And give them victory o'er the grave.

O come, Thou Dayspring, come and cheer
Our spirits by Thine advent here;
Disperse the gloomy clouds of night,
And death's dark shadows put to flight.

O come, Thou Key of David, come,
And open wide our heavenly home;
Make safe the way that leads on high,
And close the path to misery.

Each name of God embodies and represents some part of the glory of the Unseen One. In this old Latin carol the writer employs a number of names to help us see the Unseen One. Each of the lyrical appellations reflects a piece of his glory, describing for us the character and nature of Jesus. They paint a portrait of his accomplishments, authority, and power. Emmanuel—God with us. What image does that bring to mind? Imagine the Creator of the universe choosing to take on human flesh and walk among us. The Lord of Might—the awesome God who could not even be approached in ancient days, coming to draw us into his arms. Rod of Jesse—the meek, compassionate Son of God triumphs over the enemy, conquers death, and becomes a banner of life for the people. Dayspring—the Light pierces the gloom, shattering the darkness and bringing hope to those in despair. Key of David—the King opens wide the door to life and leads his subjects through to freedom.

When we comprehend the rich meaning of the titles set forth in this song, it is transformed from a simple Christmas carol into a powerful vehicle of praise and a heartfelt prayer of anticipation.

REFLECTION

By studying the names of Jesus, we learn more about him and are better able to worship him. After all, we cannot worship that which we do not know. As you look at these references, ask yourself two questions: Who is this Jesus? Why did he come? Afterwards you may find it beneficial to write your answers next to each reference.

The Lord himself will choose the sign. Look! The virgin will conceive a child! She will give birth to a son and will call him Immanuel—"God is with us."

ISAIAH 7:14

For a child is born to us, a son is given to us. And the government will rest on his shoulders. These will be his royal titles: Wonderful Counselor, Mighty God, Everlasting Father, Prince of Peace.

ISAIAH 9:6

Out of the stump of David's family will grow a shoot—yes, a new Branch bearing fruit from the old root. And the Spirit of the Lord will rest on him.

ISAIAH 11:1-2

Because of God's tender mercy, the light from heaven is about to break upon us, to give light to those who sit in darkness and in the shadow of death, and to guide us to the path of peace.

LUKE 1:78-79

I am the Alpha and the Omega—the beginning and the end, . . . the one who is, who always was, and who is still to come, the Almighty One.

REVELATION 1:8

He is the one who has the key of David. He opens doors, and no one can shut them; he shuts doors, and no one can open them.

REVELATION 3:7

PRAYER

Come now, Unseen One. Reveal to me the

wonder of your character, the splendor of your

nature, and the greatness of your name. I want to

know you.

23

CHILDREN'S SONG OF THE NATIVITY

FRANCES CHESTERTON
ENGLISH TRADITIONAL

How far is it to Bethlehem?
Not very far.
Shall we find the stable-room
Lit by a star?
Can we see the little child,
Is he within?
If we lift the wooden latch
May we go in?

May we stroke the creatures there,
Ox, ass, or sheep?

May we peep like them and see
Jesus asleep?
If we touch his tiny hand
Will he awake?
Will he know we've come so far
Just for his sake?

Great kings have precious gifts,
And we have naught,
Little smiles and little tears
Are all we brought.
For all weary children
Mary must weep.
Here, on his bed of straw
Sleep, children, sleep.

God in his mother's arms,
Babes in the byre,
Sleep, as they sleep who find
Their heart's desire.

There is such freshness in this story of the nativity. Imagine, if you will, asks Chesterton, children hearing about the birth of a Savior King. Perhaps they overheard a few shepherds excitedly discussing the event. Maybe they even saw the angels proclaiming it. However the news was passed to them, they have decided to see for themselves just what all the fuss is about. You can almost see this group of youngsters timidly entering the stable, a sense of wonder filling their hearts.

Whether or not a collection of children actually sought out the Lord at his birth, their saga is representative of us today. As Jesus said, "Unless you change and become like little children, you will never enter the kingdom of heaven." How do we change? How do we become like children? This song helps answer those questions.

Notice the language the writer uses—shall we find? can we see? may we peep? will he know? Such child-like phrases—always asking, always curious, ever seeking. These young ones seem quite aware that they have no right to be there. They realize that they bring no great gifts, only tears and smiles. Yet they enter in, hoping to see him, wanting to touch him and share his bed of straw. Isn't this just how Jesus asks us to approach him—in humility, innocence, and awe? Such is the worship that he esteems.

REFLECTION

Throughout Scripture God refers to us as children. Whose children we are and whether we act childish or childlike is a choice that is left up to us. The following passage describes what it means to live as children of God.

Live no longer as the ungodly do, for they are hopelessly confused. Their closed minds are full of darkness. Throw off your old evil nature and your former way of life, which is rotten through and through, full of lust and deception. Instead, there must be a spiritual renewal of your thoughts and attitudes. You must display a new nature because you are a new person, created in God's likeness—righteous, holy, and true.

So put away all falsehood and "tell your neighbor the truth" because we belong to each other. And "don't sin by letting anger gain control over you." Don't let the sun go down while you are still angry, for anger gives a mighty foothold to the Devil.

If you are a thief, stop stealing. Begin using your hands for
honest work, and then give generously to others in need.
Don't use foul or abusive language. Let everything you say
be good and helpful, so that your words will be an
encouragement to those who hear them.

Get rid of all bitterness, rage, anger, harsh words, and slander,
as well as all types of malicious behavior. Instead, be kind
to each other, tenderhearted, forgiving one another,
just as God through Christ has forgiven you.

Follow God's example in everything you do, because you are his
dear children. Live a life filled with love for others, following the
example of Christ, who loved you and gave himself as a sacrifice
to take away your sins.

EPHESIANS 4:17-18, 22-29, 31—5:2

PRAYER

Ask God to empower you to live as his child,

ever seeking after him with a pure heart. Invite his

Spirit to root out childishness and all of its selfish

manifestations. Commit yourself to serve him

humbly in childlike reverence. Ask him to bear

the fruit of light in you—goodness, righteousness,

and truth.

O COME, ALL YE FAITHFUL

LATIN, EIGHTEENTH CENTURY
TRANSLATED BY FREDERICK OAKELEY, 1852

O come, all ye faithful, joyful and triumphant,
O come ye, O come ye to Bethlehem!
Come and behold Him, born the King of angels!

O come, let us adore Him,
O come, let us adore Him,
O come, let us adore Him,
Christ the Lord!

The brightness of glory, Light of light eternal,
Our lowly nature He hath not abhorred:
Son of the Father, Word of God incarnate!

Sing, choirs of angels, sing in exultation,
O sing, all ye citizens of heaven above!
Glory to God, glory in the highest!

Yea, Lord, we greet Thee, born this happy morning;
Jesus, to Thee be all glory given;
Word of the Father, now in flesh appearing!

In sending Jesus to earth, the Father set out to establish a new covenant with humankind. Through the shed blood of his Son, God established a new and living way for us to fellowship with him. Instead of offering bulls and sheep on an ancient altar, we have only to call on the name of Jesus and rely on the blood he shed for us to enter into the very presence of almighty God.

When God made covenants with individuals in the Old Testament, he often changed their name. Abram (exalted father) became Abraham (father of a multitude), Jacob (supplanter) became Israel (prince with God). In each case their name was changed to reflect their change of character and their new relationship with God. We of the new covenant in Jesus have also gained a new identity. Having been "born again" by the Spirit, we are transformed from sinners to saints, from disobedient rebels to faithful followers of God. We who were once far off are drawn near his throne of grace as sons and daughters.

The Father's heart as expressed in this song cries out to us: "Come, faithful ones. Come, you joyful and triumphant ones. Come and look upon the King of angels. Behold the brightness of his glory, the light of his eternal fire. Come," the Father gently beckons, "come, you who have become my children, and give glory to my Son."

Our response, found in the final stanza and the refrain, is to gladly welcome him and lift up a chorus of joyous praise and adoration.

REFLECTION

To adore literally means to "put the mouth to, or kiss, in worship." In past centuries adoration was expressed to dignitaries and rulers by bowing and kissing their ring or feet. We find the same activity spoken of in the Bible. The Greek word for worship, *proskuneo* (see John 4:23-24), is defined as giving reverence by turning towards and kissing. It implies a humble attitude or posture, a total focus on the object of worship, and a special intimacy. With that in mind, allow these verses to spur you toward adoring him.

Exalt the Lord our God! Bow low before his feet, for he is holy!

PSALM 99:5

Honor and majesty surround him; strength and beauty are in his dwelling. O nations of the world, recognize the Lord, recognize that the Lord is glorious and strong. Give to the Lord the glory he deserves! Bring your offering and come to worship him. Worship the Lord in all his holy splendor.

1 CHRONICLES 16:27-29

Come, let us worship and bow down. Let us kneel before the Lord our maker, for he is our God.

PSALM 95:6-7

PRAYER

Worshiping you is such a privilege, Lord. To look into your eyes, to tell you how much I love you, to kiss your face . . . Though I am unworthy to enjoy such intimacy with a holy God, I come boldly, confidently before your throne through the blood of your Son. Allow me to bask here in your presence while I make my adoration for you known.

25

WE WOULD SEE JESUS

J. EDGAR PARK, 1913

We would see Jesus; lo! His star is shining
Above the stable while the angels sing;
There in a manger on the hay reclining,
Haste, let us lay our gifts before the King.

We would see Jesus, Mary's Son most holy,
Light of the village life from day to day,
Shining revealed through every task most lowly,
The Christ of God, the Life, the Truth, the Way.

We would see Jesus on the mountain teaching,
With all the listening people gathered round;
While birds and flowers and sky above are preaching
The blessedness which simple trust has found.

We would see Jesus; in the early morning,
Still as of old he calleth, "Follow Me";
Let us arise, all meaner service scorning;
Lord, we are Thine, we give ourselves to Thee.

This carol expresses the deep yearning of all who hunger for God. Its repeating first line is the heart cry of those who seek after truth. The phrase "we would see Jesus" finds its origin in the Gospel of John. According to the apostle's account, a group of Greeks had journeyed to Jerusalem in order to worship. These fellows approached Philip, one of the disciples, and made a request: "Sir, we wish to see Jesus."

Seeing Jesus should be our primary goal in worship. As Judson Cornwall once wrote, "worship without an awareness of Christ is impossible. . . . For to behold Him is to love Him, and to love Him is to worship Him." Singing, praying, serving, and even living are meaningless if we fail to recognize Jesus as our source, the cause and object of our devotion. To look up into his radiant face and gaze into his merciful eyes is to know love beyond compare.

REFLECTION

The Greeks who sought Jesus wanted to physically see him. Unfortunately, until he returns, we will not be afforded that opportunity. We can, however, look upon him with spiritual eyes. The following verses speak about how this supernatural sight can be honed.

Desire

The one thing I ask of the Lord—the thing I seek most—
is to live in the house of the Lord all the days of my life,
delighting in the Lord's perfections and
meditating in his Temple.

PSALM 27:4

Initiative

I lift my eyes to you, O God, enthroned in heaven.
We look to the Lord our God for his mercy, just as servants
keep their eyes on their master, as a slave girl watches her
mistress for the slightest signal.

PSALM 123:1-2

Persistence

My eyes are always looking to the Lord for help, for he alone can rescue me from the traps of my enemies.

I look to you for help, O Sovereign Lord. You are my refuge.

PSALMS 25:15; 141:8

Purity

God blesses those whose hearts are pure, for they will see God.

MATTHEW 5:8

PRAYER

Father, this song reflects my deepest prayer: that I may clearly see your Son. Purify my heart and restore sight to my blind eyes. Let me now see him, know him, and love him. Like the psalmist, I fix my gaze on Jesus, the focus of my worship. As I humbly follow after him, let others see Jesus in me.

26

HARK! THE HERALD ANGELS SING

CHARLES WESLEY, 1739

Hark! the herald angels sing,
"Glory to the newborn King;
Peace on earth, and mercy mild,
God and sinners reconciled!"
Joyful, all ye nations, rise,
Join the triumph of the skies;
With th' angelic host proclaim,
"Christ is born in Bethlehem!"

Hark! the herald angels sing,
"Glory to the newborn King!"

Christ, by highest heaven adored;
Christ, the everlasting Lord!

Late in time behold Him come,
Offspring of a virgin's womb.
Veiled in flesh the Godhead see;
Hail th' incarnate Deity,
Pleased as man with men to dwell,
Jesus, our Emmanuel.

Hail, the heav'n-born Prince of Peace!
Hail, the Sun of Righteousness!
Light and life to all He brings,
Ris'n with healing in His wings.
Mild He lays His glory by,
Born that man no more may die,
Born to raise the sons of earth,
Born to give them second birth.

It is obvious that the author of this song had a keen appreciation and understanding of God and his purposes. Hymn writer Charles Wesley offers us a study on the names of Jesus and the mystery of his incarnation. King, Lord, Emmanuel, Prince of Peace, Sun of Righteousness . . . all these names find their origin in Scripture and reflect a facet of the Savior's character and position.

Who is this Jesus and why did he come? Wesley answers these questions with vivid word pictures. In the first stanza he announces that Jesus came to reconcile God and mankind. No more would sin divide the two. In the next stanza he describes Jesus as the fullness of the Godhead veiled in flesh, the "incarnate Deity." In the final verses, he explains that Jesus brought with him light, life, and healing, as well as an end to death. This powerful message is good reason for us to give "glory to the newborn King."

REFLECTION

Read through the Scriptures below and then reread the words to Wesley's song.

Christ is the visible image of the invisible God. He existed before God made anything at all and is supreme over all creation. Christ is the one through whom God created everything in heaven and earth. He made the things we can see and the things we can't see—kings, kingdoms, rulers, and authorities. Everything has

been created through him and for him. He existed before
everything else began, and he holds all creation together.

Christ is the head of the church, which is his body. He is the first
of all who will rise from the dead, so he is first in everything.
For God in all his fullness was pleased to live in Christ, and by
him God reconciled everything to himself. He made peace with
everything in heaven and on earth by means of his blood on
the cross. This includes you who were once so far away
from God. You were his enemies, separated from him by your
evil thoughts and actions, yet now he has brought you back as his
friends. He has done this through his death on the cross in his
own human body. As a result, he has brought you into the very
presence of God, and you are holy and blameless as you stand
before him without a single fault.

COLOSSIANS 1:15-22

146

PRAYER

"Hail" means to welcome or greet with cheers and acclaim. That is how I respond to you this day, Jesus. I hail you, Prince of Peace, Sun of Righteousness! Bestow upon me your light, life, and healing, as I bow and give glory to your name.

27

CHRISTMAS HYMN

AMY GRANT, 1983

Praise to God whose love was shown,
Who sent his Son to earth.
Jesus left his rightful throne,
Became a man by birth.

The virgin's baby son,
All creation praised;
God incarnate come,
Come to Bethlehem.

Still a higher call had He,
Deliverance from our sins—
Come to set all people free
From Satan's hold within.

For by the sin of man we fell;
By the Son of God
He crushed the power of hell—
Death we fear no more.

Now we stand with strength, with power,
The sons of God on earth,
Faithful to the final hour,
Christ's righteousness our worth.

And now all praise is given,
For the babe, the Son,
The Savior King is risen,
Christ is Lord indeed.

This contemporary Christmas hymn is a power-ful declaration of faith. Grant invites us to join her in professing what we believe. Each verse adds to the last until the foundations of faith have been laid.

The first two verses answer the why of Jesus' birth: because of God's love. The next two deal with the why of his mission: to deliver us from sin, death, hell, and the devil. The fifth verse is a triumphant proclamation of our standing in Christ: sons of God in righteousness. The final verse is the necessary call for praise to be lifted up to the one who lived, died, and rose again.

Consider the power, freedom, and joy which now belongs to those who hope in the living God. Speak the lyrics aloud. Let them become a statement of what you know to be true. Take courage from them, and allow them to increase your faith.

REFLECTION

One day in the not too distant future God's people will stand before his throne and sing together endless songs of praise. This song may even be among those wafting through heaven for all eternity. In any case, the Bible gives us a glimpse of what that day will be like.

I looked and I saw a Lamb that had been killed but was now standing between the throne and the four living beings and among the twenty-four elders. He had seven horns and seven eyes, which are the seven spirits of God that are sent out into every part of the earth. He stepped forward and took the scroll from the right hand of the one sitting on the throne. And as he took the scroll, the four living beings and the twenty-four elders fell down before the Lamb. Each one had a harp, and they held gold bowls filled with incense—the prayers of God's people!

And they sang a new song with these words: "You are worthy to take the scroll and break its seals and open it. For you were killed, and your blood has ransomed people for God from every tribe and language and people and nation. And you have caused them to become God's Kingdom and his priests. And they will reign on the earth."

Then I looked again, and I heard the singing of thousands and millions of angels around the throne and the living beings and the elders. And they sang in a mighty chorus: "The Lamb is worthy—the Lamb who was killed. He is worthy to receive power and riches and wisdom and strength and honor and glory and blessing."

And then I heard every creature in heaven and on earth and under the earth and in the sea. They also sang: "Blessing and honor and glory and power belong to the one sitting on the throne and to the Lamb forever and ever."

REVELATION 5:6-13

PRAYER

*F*ather, *how I look forward to the wondrous cel-*

ebration which will take place before your

throne. Yet I cannot put off my desire to express

praise to you. I must begin my song now. Unto

you and to the Lamb, I lift all praise, honor, glory,

and power, for ever and ever!

JOY TO THE WORLD!

ISAAC WATTS, 1719

Joy to the world! the Lord is come;
Let earth receive her King;
Let every heart prepare Him room,
And heaven and nature sing.

Joy to the earth! the Savior reigns;
Let men their songs employ;
While fields and floods, rocks, hills and plains
Repeat the sounding joy.

He rules the world with truth and grace,
And makes the nations prove
The glories of His righteousness,
And wonders of His love.

In this carol, based loosely on Psalm 98, the great hymn writer Isaac Watts captures the spirit of celebration that Christmas should evoke in all of us. The Lord of the universe has come, and he has set us free. Where once sin, death, and the devil reigned, Jesus now reigns. We certainly have cause to celebrate. At Watts's urging, let's break out the instruments, lift up a song, and praise God by dancing and making a joyful noise.

REFLECTION

Celebration is one of the major themes of the Psalms. In the Psalms we find many patterns for rejoicing before God. As you read these examples, ask the Lord to release you to make a joyful noise to him. Then "just do it!"

Sing a new song to the Lord, for he has done wonderful deeds. He has won a mighty victory by his power and holiness. Shout to the Lord, all the earth; break out in praise and sing for joy! Sing your praise to the Lord with the harp, with the harp and melodious

song, with trumpets and the sound of the ram's horn. Make a
joyful symphony before the Lord, the King!

PSALM 98:1, 4-6

Praise God in his heavenly dwelling; praise him in his mighty
heaven! Praise him for his mighty works; praise his unequaled
greatness! Praise him with a blast of the trumpet; praise him with
the lyre and harp! Praise him with the tambourine and dancing;
praise him with stringed instruments and flutes! Praise him with
a clash of cymbals; praise him with loud clanging cymbals. Let
everything that lives sing praises to the Lord! Praise the Lord!

PSALM 150

PRAYER

Jesus, you have made me glad. Your coming has
given me reason to rejoice. I joyfully declare that
you are King. Prepare my heart to receive all that
you are and have for me. Come and take up resi-
dence there.

How Lovely Shines the Morning Star!

PHILIPP NICOLAI, 1597

How lovely shines the Morning Star!
The nations see and hail afar
The light in Judah shining.
Thou David's Son of Jacob's race,
My Bridegroom and my King of Grace,
For Thee my heart is pining.
Lowly, holy, great and glorious,
Thou victorious Prince of graces,
Filling all the heavenly places.

O highest joy by mortals won,
True Son of God and Mary's Son,
Thou high-born King of ages!

Thou art my heart's most beauteous Flower,
And Thy blest gospel's saving power
My raptured soul engages.
Thou mine, I Thine; Sing Hosanna!
Heavenly manna, tasting, eating,
Whilst Thy love in songs repeating.

A pledge of peace from God I see
When Thy pure eyes are turned to me
To show me thy good pleasure.
Jesus, Thy Spirit and Thy Word,
Thy body and Thy blood afford
My soul its dearest treasure.
Keep me kindly in Thy favor,
O my Savior! Thou wilt cheer me;
Thy Word calls me to draw near Thee.

Oh, joy to know that Thou, my Friend,
Art Lord, Beginning without end,
The First and Last, Eternal!
And Thou at length, O glorious grace,
Wilt take me to that holy place,
The home of joys supernal.

Amen, Amen! Come and meet me!
Quickly greet me! With deep yearning,
Lord, I look for Thy returning.

What a powerful anthem of praise! Had it not been set to music, this poem by Philipp Nicolai would still remain a stirring and worthy tribute to the Lord. Its striking imagery, rich theological themes, and skillful use of Christ's titles make it a classic hymn.

Think of it as a sumptuous feast—filled with spiritual appetizers, entrees, side dishes, and desserts. To rush through it would be an insult to chef Nicolai. Take time to savor it. Read it carefully, consider the theme, and make notes about those lines and phrases the Lord impresses upon you. Written in first person, it also lends itself to reading aloud as a prayer of praise.

REFLECTION

It is amazing how wonderfully complex Jesus is. The God/Man, fully God, fully man . . . such mysteries are too much for our finite minds to fully grasp. Even the most creative artists and musicians have a difficult time communicating all that he is. The following verses show us just how incredible, how awesome this Jesus is. As you read them, ask the Lord to expand your understanding and reveal the truth and reality of his character to you.

In the beginning the Word already existed. He was with God, and he was God. He was in the beginning with God. He created everything there is. Nothing exists that he didn't make. Life itself was in him, and this life gives light to everyone. The light shines through the darkness, and the darkness can never extinguish it.

JOHN 1:1-5

I pray that you will begin to understand the incredible greatness of his power for us who believe him. This is the same mighty power that raised Christ from the dead and seated him in the place of honor at God's right hand in the heavenly realms. Now he is far above any ruler or authority or power or leader or anything else in this world or in the world to come. And God has put all things under the authority of Christ, and he gave him this authority for the benefit of the church. And the church is his

body; it is filled by Christ, who fills everything everywhere with
his presence.

EPHESIANS 1:19-23

Long ago God spoke many times and in many ways to our
ancestors through the prophets. But now in these final days, he
has spoken to us through his Son. God promised everything to the
Son as an inheritance, and through the Son he made the universe
and everything in it. The Son reflects God's own glory, and
everything about him represents God exactly. He sustains the
universe by the mighty power of his command. After he died to
cleanse us from the stain of sin, he sat down in the place of honor
at the right hand of the majestic God of heaven. This shows that
God's Son is far greater than the angels, just as the name God
gave him is far greater than their names.

HEBREWS 1:1-4

When I turned to see who was speaking to me, I saw seven gold
lampstands. And standing in the middle of the lampstands was
the Son of Man. He was wearing a long robe with a gold sash
across his chest. His head and his hair were white like wool, as
white as snow. And his eyes were bright like flames of fire. His
feet were as bright as bronze refined in a furnace, and his voice

thundered like mighty ocean waves. He held seven stars in his right hand, and a sharp two-edged sword came from his mouth. And his face was as bright as the sun in all its brilliance. When I saw him, I fell at his feet as dead. But he laid his right hand on me and said, "Don't be afraid! I am the First and the Last. I am the living one who died. Look, I am alive forever and ever! And I hold the keys of death and the grave."

REVELATION 1:12-18

PRAYER

When I comprehend even the smallest fragment of your greatness, Lord, my knees begin to wobble. In your presence I, like John, am suddenly aware of how weak and powerless I truly am. Today I throw myself at your feet "as dead." For I have, in fact, died to self and sin and been reborn. My life is now in you. Do with me as you desire.

WE THREE KINGS

JOHN HENRY HOPKINS, 1857

We three kings of Orient are;
Bearing gifts we traverse afar,
Field and fountain, moor and mountain,
Following yonder star.

O star of wonder, star of night,
Star with royal beauty bright,
Westward leading, still proceeding,
Guide us to thy perfect light.

Born a King on Bethlehem's plain,
Gold I bring to crown Him again,
King forever, ceasing never
Over us all to reign.

Frankincense to offer have I;
Incense owns a Deity nigh;
Prayer and praising all men raising,
Worship Him, God on high.

Myrrh is mine; its bitter perfume
Breathes a life of gathering gloom:
Sorrowing, sighing, bleeding, dying,
Sealed in the stone-cold tomb.

Glorious now behold Him arise,
King and God and Sacrifice;
Alleluia, alleluia!
Earth to heav'n replies.

In creating this popular song, John Henry Hopkins skillfully wove together swatches of Scripture, church tradition, and legend. The Bible actually tells us very little about the men who came from the East to visit Christ. It never mentions how many there were, their names, or that they were, in fact, kings. It simply calls them "magi." Some Bible scholars believe that this term refers to a caste of Persian priests or sorcerers who were experts in astrology, divination, and the interpretation of dreams. While they could have been rulers of a sort because of their priestly offices, we have no reason to believe that they possessed great wealth.

What we do know is that these Gentiles traveled some distance, intent upon worshiping the newborn King of the Jews. With them they brought gifts of great worth. As Hopkins poetically explains, these gifts foretold who and what this child would be. Gold prophesied of his kingship. The frankincense spoke of the purity of his life. Myrrh, a spice used to embalm the dead, predicted his coming death.

Viewed from another angle, these gifts comprise that which the Lord desires us to offer him today. The gold symbolizes our most precious treasures, our hopes and dreams. When we give these to Jesus, we are giving him our heart. The frankincense denotes the pleasing fragrance that arises from a life of holiness. Here we offer him our obedience. The myrrh proclaims the fact that we have died to self and that we now live to Christ. It means giving him our very life.

REFLECTION

Let these words aid you in preparing your gifts for the King.

Wherever your treasure is, there your heart and thoughts will also be.

LUKE 12:34

You must be holy in everything you do, just as God—who chose you to be his children—is holy.

1 PETER 1:15

If any of you wants to be my follower, you must put aside your selfish ambition, shoulder your cross daily, and follow me. If you try to keep your life for yourself, you will lose it. But if you give up your life for me, you will find true life.

LUKE 9:23-25

PRAYER

I pledge my heart, my obedience, and the title deed of my life to you, Jesus. I approach you like the wise men, intent on worshiping with these gifts outstretched to you. "May the words of my mouth and the meditation of my heart be pleasing in your sight, O Lord, my Rock and my Redeemer" (Psalm 19:14, NIV).

ALL PRAISE TO JESUS

C. A. LANE, 1990

Messengers from the heavenly sphere
Spreading news of joy and cheer
That to us a Child was born,
The Lord disguised in earthly form.

All praise to Jesus, King of Kings,
To you all of creation sings:
Messiah, the Anointed One,
Prince of Peace, God's only Son.

Humbly your life here began,
Yet with power, a sovereign plan
To deliver men from chains,
From devil's tempting, from death's pains.

On the cross your blood was shed
As you suffered in our stead;
Your love won our victory,
Loosing bonds to set us free.

Out of death you rose with power
In your resurrection hour;
The gates of life you swung full wide
And bid us follow you inside.

We who have now seen your light
Celebrate this holy night;
With glad hearts we shout and sing
Praise to you, our risen King!

Have you ever wondered why Christmas is so widely accepted? Think about it for a moment. What other holiday is celebrated the world over by multitudes of people from diverse religious and cultural backgrounds? Not Good Friday. Not Easter. Not Ascension Day or Pentecost. Christmas is the only day that has been transformed into a global extravaganza. Why? Because Christmas is safe.

The other "holy days" on the Christian calendar are confrontational. They straightforwardly demand that we affirm or reject a belief in Jesus' death and resurrection, his lordship, authority, and power. But Christmas is simply the story of a baby. Who could be offended by that? That it took place in a barn in Bethlehem and involved animals, shepherds, a star, and three mysterious guests simply adds to the magical quality of the account.

Were the real message of Christmas to break through this fairy-tale-like facade for even an instant, it would quickly become a most unpopular holiday. For at its center, Christmas asks two difficult questions: Who is Jesus? Why was he born? It's one thing to smile at the innocent child in the nativity scene and quite another to consider that he is the only Son of God, come to reconcile man to his Creator.

Perhaps the world does recognize the true meaning of Christmas. That would explain why many people go to such great lengths to detach this holiday from the one it is intended to honor. What these poor souls fail to understand is that Christmas cannot be celebrated outside of Christ. The idea is absurd, like holding a party without inviting the guest of honor. There's no way around it. Christmas is for, about, and finds its fulfillment in Jesus.

REFLECTION

Let the following verses become your confession of faith. Use them to offer up thanks and praise to the one in whom you believe.

When Jesus came to the region of Caesarea Philippi, he asked his disciples, "Who do people say that the Son of Man is?"

"Well," they replied, "some say John the Baptist, some say Elijah, and others say Jeremiah or one of the other prophets."

Then he asked them, "Who do you say I am?"

Simon Peter answered, "You are the Messiah, the Son of the living God."

MATTHEW 16:13-16

174

*I am the way, the truth, and the life. No one can come to the
Father except through me.*

JOHN 14:6

*I am the resurrection and the life. Those who believe in me, even
though they die like everyone else, will live again.*

JOHN 11:25

# PRAYER

Lord, I have seen your light. With a glad heart I

come to celebrate, shouting and singing my

praise to you. Jesus, you are the King of kings.

You are Messiah, the Anointed One. I bow down

before you, Prince of Peace. I confess that you are

God's only Son. All honor and glory be unto you

forever and ever. Amen.

BIBLIOGRAPHY

Cornwall, Judson. *Elements of Worship.* South Plainfield, N.J.: Bridge Publishing Inc., 1985.

Del Re, Gerand and Patricia. *The Christmas Almanack.* Garden City, N.Y.: Doubleday & Company, Inc., 1979.

Ehret, Walter, and George K. Evans. *The International Book of Christmas Carols.* Lexington, Mass.: The Stephen Greene Press, 1980.

Emurian, Ernest K. *Stories of Christmas Carols.* Boston: W. A. Wilde Co., 1958.

Joy To The World: The Sing-Along Christmas Book. Miami Beach, Fla.: Hansen House, 1990.

Noble, Tertius T. (music arrangement); and Helen Sewell (illustrator). *A Round of Carols.* New York: Henry Z. Welck, Inc.

Robbins, Rossell Hope. *Early English Christmas Carols.* New York: Columbia University Press, 1961.

Sayre, Eleanor (editor). *A Christmas Book: Fifty Carols and Poems From the 14th to the 17th Centuries.* New York: Clarkson N. Potter, Inc., 1966.

Shipley, Joseph T. *Dictionary of Word Origins.* New York: Philosophical Library, Inc., 1945.

Today's Dictionary of the Bible. Compiled by T. A. Bryant. Carmel, N.Y.: Guideposts, 1982.

Vine, W. E. *Vine's Expository Dictionary of Old and New Testament Words.* Old Tappan, N.J.: Fleming H. Revell Company, 1981.

Wernecke, Herbert H. *Christmas Songs and Their Stories.* Philadelphia: The Westminster Press, 1957.

White, David Manning. *The Search for God.* New York: MacMillan, 1983.

The Yuletide Caroler. Minneapolis: Augsburg Publishing House, 1965.